The

"I Love Lucy"®

Cookbook

Sarah Key
Vicki Wells
Jennifer Newman Brazil

Abbeville Press Publishers
New York   London   Paris

DESIGNER: Patricia Fabricant
PRODUCTION MANAGER: Dana Cole
PRODUCTION EDITOR: Owen Dugan

Special thanks to Tom Sabatino, Mary Long, and Jean-François Coste.

Also available in the Hollywood Hotplates series:
The Casablanca Cookbook
A Christmas Carol Cookbook
Gone With The Wind Cook Book™
The Wizard of Oz™ *Cookbook*

First edition

6 8 10 9 7 5

Library of Congress Cataloging-in-Publication Data
Key, Sarah.
The I love Lucy cookbook / Sarah Key, Vicki Wells, Jennifer Newman Brazil.
p.   cm. — (Hollywood hotplates)
ISBN 1-55859-855-3
1. Cookery.   2. I love Lucy (Television program)   I. Wells, Vicki.
II. Brazil, Jennifer Newman.   III. Title.   IV. Series.
TX714.K5   1994
641.5—dc20   94-32479

METRIC CONVERSIONS: 1 teaspoon = 5 ml; 1 tablespoon = 14.8 ml.

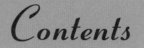

Contents

"Paris at Last"
Lucy's Lunch in Montmartre • 5

"Lucy's Italian Movie"
A Divine Dinner of "Bitter Grapes" • 15

"California, Here We Come"
A Roadside Picnic • 23

"Visitor from Italy"
Mario Gets a Little Taste of Cuba • 31

"Lucy Does a TV Commercial"
Cocktails at the Tropicana • 41

"Job Switching"
Sweets from the Chocolate Factory • 49

"L.A. at Last"
Desserts at the Brown Derby • 57

Paris
at Last

Lucy's Lunch in Montmartre

LUCY: Waiter, this food has snails in it.

WAITER: Pardon?

LUCY: Snails! Am I supposed to eat this? Maybe if I had some ketchup.

WAITER: *Sauce tomate?*

LUCY: Yeah, *sauce tomate,* lots of it. (looking at escargot) I think an American cousin of yours ate my geranium plant.

WAITER & CHEF: *Gendarme! Gendarme!*

LUCY: *Gendarme?* Police?

WAITER & CHEF: *Oui,* police! Police!

LUCY: Since when is it a crime to put ketchup on snails?

A la Porte Montmartre Escargots

1 cup (240 g) unsalted butter
1/4 cup (30 g) chopped shallots
2 tablespoons chopped garlic
1/3 cup (15 g) chopped fresh basil
1 teaspoon grated lemon zest
3 sheets of phyllo dough
12 escargots

*P*reheat oven to 375°F (190°C). In a small saucepan, melt butter. Then add shallots and garlic. Let cook slowly for 3 to 4 minutes. Remove pan from heat and stir in basil and lemon zest. Lay one sheet of phyllo on a flat work surface. Brush basil butter generously over phyllo. Place a second sheet of phyllo on top of the first sheet. Brush the surface of the second sheet of phyllo with basil butter. Repeat with a third piece of phyllo pastry. Cut phyllo evenly into 12 squares. Place 1 escargot on each square. Bring edges of phyllo up around each escargot. Twist slightly to seal, then press to form a small "beggar's purse." Place purses on a baking sheet lined with parchment or wax paper and bake for 20 to 25 minutes, until golden brown. Serve immediately.

Makes 12 hors d'oeuvres.

RICKY: *Honey, you can't go running around Paris all by yourself.*
LUCY: *Why not?*
RICKY: *What about your French?*
LUCY: *What about my French?*
RICKY: *Well, Paris is a big city, and not knowing the language, you're liable to get in a lot of trouble.*
LUCY: *Well, when you first came to the United States, you didn't get into a lot of trouble because you didn't know the language, did you?*
RICKY: *I'm married, aren't I? She told me that "I do" meant "Pleased to meet you," and then she introduced me to the preacher.*

Smoked Trout Salad with Horseradish Vinaigrette

DRESSING
3 tablespoons prepared horseradish
3 tablespoons granulated sugar
1 tablespoon Dijon mustard
¼ cup (60 ml) red wine vinegar
2 tablespoons chopped fresh dill
¾ cup (180 ml) olive oil
freshly ground black pepper to taste

SALAD
8 cups (350 g) mixed salad greens, washed, dried,
and torn into bite-sized pieces
1 cucumber, peeled and thinly sliced
½ cup (15 g) thinly sliced scallions
1 red bell pepper, seeded and thinly sliced
1 6-ounce (180-g) jar artichoke hearts, drained
½ cup (60 g) fresh shelled peas
1 pound (460 g) smoked trout fillets

To prepare dressing, whisk together horseradish, sugar, mustard, vinegar, and dill in a small bowl. Slowly drizzle olive oil into mixture while whisking continuously. Season to taste with pepper. In a large bowl, toss mixed greens with enough dressing (about ¼ cup/60 ml) to cover them lightly. Arrange greens on 4 chilled plates. Top each plate with cucumber slices, scallions, red pepper, artichoke hearts, and peas. Remove skin from trout fillets and check for any small bones. Break trout into large chunks and arrange on the 4 salads. Serve immediately with remaining salad dressing on side.

Serves 4 as a lunch or first course.

RICKY: *Are you all right?*
LUCY: *I never was so glad to hear anybody speak English in my life. Even you.*
RICKY: *What happened?*
LUCY: *I don't know. Nobody speaks English. They're all foreigners.*

Hotel Royale Steak au Poivre

2 tablespoons cracked black peppercorns
(see note below)
4 boneless strip steaks (8 ounces/230 g each),
trimmed of all fat
3 tablespoons vegetable oil
3 tablespoons minced shallots
$2/3$ cup (160 ml) heavy cream
$1/2$ teaspoon salt
2 tablespoons cognac
2 sprigs fresh thyme
1 tablespoon red wine vinegar

Spread cracked pepper on a plate. Press pepper into both sides of each steak. Meanwhile, in a large sauté pan, heat 2 tablespoons oil. Sauté steaks in hot oil over medium-high heat for about 4 minutes on each side, until cooked to desired doneness. Remove steaks to a warm serving platter and discard any oil in the pan. Add remaining tablespoon oil to pan with shallots. Sauté over medium heat for about 3 minutes. Add cream and salt. Cook for 2 minutes. Add cognac and thyme sprigs. Continue to simmer over medium heat for another 1 to 2 minutes. Add vinegar and adjust seasoning. Pour sauce over steaks. Garnish with whole peppercorns and sprigs of thyme if desired. Traditionally, steak au poivre is served with potatoes and watercress.

Note: To crack pepper, spread whole peppercorns on work surface. Press with the bottom of a heavy pan until peppercorns are crushed. Precracked pepper is also available.

Makes 4 servings.

Boyer's Bistro Onion Soup

3 tablespoons unsalted butter
2 large red onions (24 ounces/700 g),
sliced medium-thin
2 large yellow Spanish onions (24 ounces/700 g),
sliced medium-thin
2 cloves (1 tablespoon) garlic, chopped
1 tablespoon chopped shallot
1 teaspoon salt
1/4 teaspoon freshly ground black pepper
3 tablespoons flour
1 cup (240 ml) dry white wine
4 cups (1 liter) chicken broth
1/4 cup (60 ml) heavy cream
2 cups (230 g) grated Gruyère cheese

*M*elt butter in a large heavy-bottomed pot. Add onions, garlic, and shallot, and sprinkle with salt and pepper. Cover pot and cook over medium-low heat for 20 minutes, stirring occasionally. Remove cover and continue to cook until onions caramelize, stirring frequently to prevent burning. This will take 20 to 30 minutes. Turn heat to low and whisk in flour. Cook 3 more minutes, then add wine and chicken broth slowly, whisking constantly. Bring to a boil and let simmer 15 minutes, whisking occasionally. Add cream and let cook 5 more minutes. Turn heat off and add cheese, stirring with a whisk until cheese melts. Serve immediately.

Makes 6 servings.

*In "Paris at Last" the Desilu prop department made
an error by placing a bottle of California wine—
Paul Masson—on the table.
(From Bart Andrews,* The "I Love Lucy" Book, *Doubleday, 1985.)*

Parisian Waffles

1 stick (½ cup/120 g) plus 2 tablespoons
unsalted butter
1½ cups (180 g) all-purpose flour
2 teaspoons baking powder
¼ teaspoon salt
6 eggs
¾ to 1 cup (240 ml) buttermilk
¼ cup (60 ml) heavy cream
2 teaspoons grated orange zest
1 teaspoon chopped fresh sage
1 tablespoon honey
4 thick slices Canadian bacon (⅓ pound/150 g)

*M*elt the stick of butter in a small saucepan. Allow to cook for about 5 minutes, until butter becomes golden and a small amount of sediment is visible. Set aside. In a medium bowl, mix together flour, baking powder, and salt. Make a well in the center and add 2 eggs to the well. Start to whisk slowly, working out toward the edges, to mix the dry ingredients with the eggs. When about half of the flour has been mixed in, begin to add ¾ cup (180 ml) buttermilk to the center while whisking. Add cream and blend mixture until flour is just incorporated. Add melted butter, orange zest, and sage. Whisk until blended. Make waffles according to instructions for your waffle iron. This batter makes 4 medium waffles. If batter is too thick, add up to ¼ cup (60 ml) additional buttermilk. Melt honey and 2 tablespoons butter in a small saucepan and keep warm on the side. Place each cooked waffle on a plate. Meanwhile, in a large sauté pan, brown bacon over medium-high heat. Place 1 slice on each waffle. In same sauté pan, fry the remaining 4 eggs in the grease left in the pan (add a little vegetable oil if needed to prevent sticking). Season to taste with salt and pepper. Place 1 egg on each waffle on top of the bacon. Drizzle the waffles with the honey butter and serve immediately.

Note: To make a more elaborate version of this dish, use poached eggs instead of fried eggs. For a very rich variation, the poached eggs can be topped with a hollandaise sauce.

Makes 4 servings.

Potato Sack Salade Lyonnaise

2 pounds (920 g) small red potatoes
1½ teaspoons salt
1 pound (460 g) cooked French garlic sausage or kielbasa
⅔ cup (160 ml) plus 1 tablespoon olive oil
4 tablespoons white wine vinegar or tarragon vinegar
½ teaspoon freshly ground black pepper
2 tablespoons Dijon mustard
¾ cup (100 g) chopped onion
1 tablespoon chopped fresh tarragon

In a large pot, cover potatoes with cold water. Bring to a boil and add ¼ teaspoon salt to the water. Boil for 20 minutes, or until tender but firm. Meanwhile, pierce sausage skin with a fork several times. Place sausage in a sauté pan, cover with water, and simmer for 10 minutes. Remove skin from sausage, slice, and keep warm. Rinse potatoes under cold water, then peel and slice them. In a large bowl, whisk together ⅓ cup (80 ml) olive oil, 2 tablespoons vinegar, 1 teaspoon salt, ½ teaspoon pepper, and 1 tablespoon mustard. Add potatoes and combine well. Sauté onion in 1 tablespoon olive oil for about 20 minutes, or until caramelized, stirring frequently. Whisk remaining oil, vinegar, mustard, salt, and pepper into onions vigorously. Arrange potato and sausage slices on a warm plate and drizzle with warm onion vinaigrette. Serve immediately.

Makes 6 servings.

LUCY: *Listen, thanks to me you got to do something that very few Americans get to do, you got to see the inside of a French jail.*
ETHEL: *Thanks to you, we almost got to spend the rest of our lives on Devil's Island.*

Counterfeit Crème Caramel

CARAMEL
1 cup (240 g) sugar
½ cup (120 ml) water
1 teaspoon lemon juice

CUSTARD
3 cups (720 ml) milk
½ vanilla bean, halved lengthwise
1 cinnamon stick
2 strips (1 x 3 inches/2.5 x 7.5 cm each) lemon zest
2 strips (1 x 3 inches/2.5 x 7.5 cm each) orange zest
3 eggs
2 egg yolks
½ cup (120 g) sugar

To make the caramel, combine the sugar, water, and lemon juice in a small nonaluminum saucepan. Bring to a boil and let cook over medium heat until sugar turns a golden brown caramel color, about 10 to 15 minutes. Carefully pour caramel into 6 4-ounce (120-ml) ramekins and swirl to coat each ramekin completely. Empty excess caramel back into saucepan. Set ramekins aside. (Be very careful, as caramel is extremely hot and can burn skin badly. To clean saucepan, dissolve remaining caramel in hot water and bring to a boil.) Preheat the oven to 325°F (165°C). To make custard, combine milk, vanilla bean, cinnamon stick, and zests in a medium saucepan. Heat gently. When mixture begins to simmer, remove from heat and let stand ½ hour. In a small bowl, combine eggs, egg yolks, and sugar with a wire whisk. Pour in milk mixture, then strain through a fine sieve. Fill each ramekin with custard mixture. Place ramekins in a large heat-proof container such as a roasting pan. Pour hot water in pan until it comes halfway up the sides of the ramekins. Bake for about 45 to 50 minutes, or until the custards are set all the way through and do not appear to be liquid in the center when shaken gently. (Be careful not to overbake, as they will develop a pitted, scrambled-egg texture instead of a smooth, satiny one.) Remove ramekins from water bath and refrigerate for at least 1 hour. To serve, run a knife around edge of custard and invert onto a serving plate.

Makes 6 servings.

Lucy's Italian Movie

A Divine Dinner of "Bitter Grapes"

LUCY: Gee, did you hear that, honey? It's going to be called "Bitter Grapes." I wonder what part they want me for.

FRED: Oh, you're probably going to be one of the bunch.

Panzanella with Black Grapes

8 ounces (230 g) crusty Italian bread, cut into
1½-inch (4-cm) squares and allowed to become stale
1 medium red onion (4 ounces/120 g), sliced thin
2 large tomatoes (1 pound/460 g), cut into thin wedges
1 bulb fennel (8 ounces/230 g), cored and sliced thin
12 ounces (350 g) black grapes, halved and seeded
¾ cup (180 ml) extra-virgin olive oil
2 tablespoons balsamic vinegar
2 tablespoons red wine vinegar
1½ teaspoons salt
freshly ground black pepper to taste
30 leaves fresh basil, left whole, washed and dried
1 bunch arugula, washed, and dried

In a large salad bowl, combine bread, onion, tomatoes, fennel, and black grapes. In a smaller bowl, whisk together olive oil, vinegars, salt, and pepper. Pour over bread mixture and toss well. Cover bowl with plastic wrap and let sit at room temperature for 1 hour. Add basil leaves and arugula to salad bowl and toss well. Serve immediately.

Makes 6 servings.

Grape Leaves Stuffed with Couscous

4 ounces (120 g) couscous
1/2 ounce (1/4 cup/30 g) pine nuts, toasted in a 400°F
(200°C) oven for 9 to 10 minutes, or until golden
1/4 cup (60 ml) plus 2 tablespoons extra-virgin olive oil
1/2 teaspoon grated orange zest
1 tablespoon freshly squeezed orange juice
2 tablespoons dried mint, crumbled
2 tablespoons chopped fresh basil
1 teaspoon salt
1/2 teaspoon freshly ground black pepper
18 vine leaves, rinsed under cold water and
dried between paper towels (see note below)
2 tablespoons freshly squeezed lemon juice
1/2 cup (120 ml) chicken broth or water

In a small bowl, soak couscous in cold water to cover for 1 minute. Drain, then dry couscous between paper towels. Return couscous to a dry bowl. Add pine nuts, 2 tablespoons olive oil, orange zest, orange juice, 1 tablespoon mint, 1 tablespoon basil, 1/2 teaspoon salt, and 1/4 teaspoon pepper. Combine well. Place a heaping tablespoon of filling in the center of each vine leaf. Roll up each leaf tightly, folding sides inward to form an egg-roll shape. Squeeze each leaf gently before placing seam side down in a medium sauté or frying pan. Pack stuffed leaves closely in 1 layer on bottom of pan. Sprinkle with remaining salt, pepper, basil, mint, and 1 tablespoon of the lemon juice. Pour broth or water over leaves. Place a plate over leaves large enough to cover all of them but small enough to fit inside pan and act as a weight. Simmer for 10 minutes. Remove grape leaves to a clean container. Drizzle with remaining olive oil and lemon juice. Chill. Serve cold as an hors d'oeuvre.

Note: Vine leaves are available in specialty or gourmet stores. They are sold in jars packed in brine.

Makes 18 stuffed grape leaves.

Lucy's "Big Pizza Feet" Foccacia

*

½ cup (50 g) currants
½ cup (120 ml) white or red wine
1 package active dry yeast
1 teaspoon sugar
2 cups (500 ml) warm water
5 cups (650 g) all-purpose flour
1 teaspoon salt
3 tablespoons extra-virgin olive oil
1 tablespoon chopped fresh rosemary
1 tablespoon cornmeal
1 medium onion (100 g), thinly sliced
1 tablespoon coarse salt (optional)

*I*n a small, nonaluminum saucepan, combine currants and wine. Heat gently to boiling, then set aside. In a large bowl, combine yeast, sugar, and ½ cup (120 ml) of the warm water. Stir to dissolve yeast. Let mixture sit until yeast starts to bubble, about 5 minutes. Add remaining water, flour, salt, and 1 tablespoon of the olive oil. Mix with a wooden spoon until a dough is formed and then add drained currants and rosemary. Turn dough out onto a floured surface and knead by hand for 10 minutes. (Alternatively, knead dough in a mixer with a dough hook or process for 4 minutes in a food processor.) Place dough in a greased large bowl, cover with plastic wrap, and let rise in a warm place until doubled in volume, about 1 to 1½ hours. Preheat oven to 450°F (230°C). Punch dough down and let rise again until doubled. Sprinkle a 12 × 18-inch (30.5 × 46-cm) baking sheet with cornmeal. Turn dough out onto sheet and spread with hands to cover sheet evenly with the dough. Brush dough with the remaining olive oil. Let rise for 10 to 15 minutes in a warm place. Dimple dough gently with fingertips and cover it evenly with slices of onions. Sprinkle with coarse salt if desired. Bake until golden brown, about 30 to 35 minutes. Serve warm or at room temperature.

Makes 1 loaf.

LUCY: *Oh, Señor Fellipi.*

VITTORIO: *How do you do?*

LUCY: *You'll have to excuse the way I look, but I've been working in the grape vineyards, so I could get the proper atmosphere for working in your picture.*

FRED: *Boy, when it comes to soaking up local color, you don't mess around.*

RICKY: *Lucy, why don't you wash that blue stuff off?*

LUCY: *I tried to. It won't come off.*

Fellipi's Fettucine with Grappa Sauce

1 tablespoon olive oil
2 medium cloves garlic, chopped
15 sun-dried tomatoes (3 ounces/90 g), packed in olive oil
1/2 cup (120 ml) grappa or brandy
1 large fresh tomato, submerged in boiling water 1 minute, then peeled, seeded, and chopped
1 teaspoon salt
1 1/2 cups (360 g) tomato purée
1 1/4 cups (300 ml) water
1/2 cup (120 ml) heavy cream
1 cup (120 g) grated Parmesan cheese
1 pound (460 g) fettucine, fresh if possible

*I*n a large heavy-bottomed saucepan, heat olive oil over medium heat. Add garlic and sauté 1 minute. Add sun-dried tomatoes and sauté 2 more minutes. Pour in grappa or brandy and reduce by half. Add chopped tomato, salt, tomato purée, and water. Cook 15 minutes. Add heavy cream and cook 5 more minutes. Turn heat off and purée sauce in a blender or food processor. Return to pot and stir in grated cheese. Cook fettucine in boiling salted water. Drain, then add to pot of sauce, and toss well to coat fettucine.

Makes 6 first course servings.

Teresa's Tuna with Caper-Raisin Butter

¼ cup (40 g) golden raisins
2 tablespoons balsamic vinegar
2 tablespoons water
1 tablespoon chopped shallots
1½ teaspoons sugar
1½ tablespoons capers, packed in salt
(or capers packed in brine, drained,
plus ¼ teaspoon salt)
½ cup (120 g) unsalted butter, at room temperature
¼ cup (60 ml) olive oil
6 tuna steaks, 1 inch thick
salt and freshly ground black pepper

Combine raisins, vinegar, water, shallots, sugar, and capers in
a small nonaluminum saucepan. Bring to a boil and reduce by
half. Remove from heat and let cool. Chop mixture by hand to a
paste or blend in a blender for a few seconds. In a medium bowl,
cream butter well with an electric mixer. Stir in cooled raisin
mixture. Form butter into a log 1½ inches (4 cm) in diameter by
rolling it in plastic wrap or wax paper. Chill until solid. Heat 1 or
2 large sauté pans until very hot and brush with olive oil. Season
tuna steaks on each side with salt and pepper. Sear tuna steaks

2 minutes on each side. Slice butter ⅛ inch (3 mm) thick. Place 2 or 3 slices on top of each hot tuna steak. Serve immediately.

Makes 6 servings.

RICKY: *Look honey, Italy has enough problems already. I don't want to have to worry about you lousing up the entire grape industry.*

LUCY: *Oh, all I want to do is soak up a little local color, so I'll know what I'm acting about. What could possibly happen to me?*

RICKY: *Well, I could answer that but we're only going to be here ten days.*

Wine-Soaked Pears

6 pears, preferably Bosc
6 cups (1.5 liters) pinot grigio or other Italian dry white wine
½ cup (120 g) sugar
1 vanilla bean, split lengthwise
juice of 1 lemon, plus 1 strip lemon zest
juice of 1 orange, plus 1 strip orange zest

Peel pears and, using a paring knife, cut out core from the bottom, leaving on stems. Slice off a thin piece from bottom to ensure they sit upright. Place pears in a nonaluminum saucepan just large enough to hold all of them standing upright. Add remaining ingredients to saucepan, scraping vanilla bean into wine. Bring to a boil, then lower heat. Poach over very low heat until pears are tender but not overly soft. This will take anywhere from ½ hour to 1½ hours, depending on ripeness of pears. Remove pears from liquid carefully and place on serving platter. Turn heat up to high and reduce wine to ¾ cup (180 ml). Strain wine glaze into a clean container and let cool 10 to 15 minutes. Pour some glaze over each pear and serve immediately.

Makes 6 servings.

California, Here We Come

A Roadside Picnic

ETHEL: What does your letter say?

LUCY: "Dear Lucy, how are you and Mickey? I couldn't find your address, so I am sending this to Ethel Mertz. If you don't get it, please let me know as I have made a copy of it." Well, that's thinking. "The copy is enclosed. As a matter of fact, if you have read this far, you must have received this letter, so tear up the copy and thank Ethel for me."

"Mickey's" Spicy Latin Lemonade

4½ cups (1.1 liters) water
¾ cup (180 g) sugar
2 cinnamon sticks, broken in half
8 whole cloves
8 whole allspice
2 star anise (optional)
1¼ cups (300 ml) freshly squeezed lemon juice
(about 10 lemons)

*I*n a medium pot, combine water, sugar, cinnamon sticks, cloves, allspice, and star anise if using. Bring to a boil and then immediately remove from heat. Let steep 1 hour. Add lemon juice and strain into a pitcher. Chill. Pour over ice to serve.

Makes 1½ quarts (1.5 liters).

Cadillac Coleslaw

1 small head cabbage (1 pound/460 g), shredded
2 teaspoons salt
2 tablespoons white vinegar
1 cup (120 g) chopped red onion
1 red bell pepper (5 ounces/150 g), chopped
2 tablespoons honey
1 teaspoon freshly ground black pepper
½ cup (120 g) mayonnaise
¼ cup (60 g) plain yogurt
2 teaspoons crushed coriander seeds (optional)

*I*n a large bowl, combine cabbage, salt, and vinegar. Let marinate 10 minutes. Add remaining ingredients and mix well. Serve at room temperature.

Makes 6 servings.

Ethel Mae's
Albuquerque Spoonbread

1½ cups (225 g) yellow cornmeal
½ teaspoon salt
¼ teaspoon cayenne pepper
½ teaspoon baking soda
2 teaspoons baking powder
3 eggs
1 cup (240 g) sour cream
1 cup (240 ml) milk
2½ tablespoons unsalted butter, melted
2 cups (240 g) fresh or
frozen (12-ounce package) corn kernels
2 cups (240 g) grated Cheddar cheese
2 to 3 pickled jalapeño peppers, minced (optional)

*P*reheat oven to 350°F (180°C). Butter an 9 × 13-inch (23 × 33-cm) baking dish. In a large bowl, combine cornmeal, salt, cayenne, baking soda, and baking powder. In another bowl, whisk together eggs, sour cream, and milk. With a wooden spoon or spatula, stir egg mixture into cornmeal mixture. Stir in melted butter, then stir in corn, cheese, and jalapeño peppers if using. Spoon mixture into prepared baking dish. Bake 35 to 40 minutes, or until a toothpick inserted in center comes out with moist crumbs. Cut into squares and, if taking on a picnic, wrap in foil while still warm.

Makes 8 servings.

Vivian Vance was raised in Albuquerque, New Mexico, and became the star player in the town's Little Theater. Born Vivian Roberta Jones, her stage name was from her dramatics teacher, Vance Randolph.
From Bart Andrews, The "I Love Lucy" Book, *Doubleday, 1985.)*

Mrs. McGillicuddy's Rice and Red Bean Salad

2 cups (400 g) cooked rice
1 10-ounce (300-g) can kidney beans, drained
1 cup (90 g) fresh or frozen corn kernels
3/4 cup (2 1/2 ounces/100 g) chopped black olives
4 tablespoons chopped fresh coriander (cilantro)
3 scallions, including green part, chopped
1 tablespoon toasted sesame seeds
1/4 cup (60 ml) freshly squeezed lime juice
1/3 cup (80 ml) olive oil
1 teaspoon soy sauce
1 teaspoon salt

Combine rice, kidney beans, corn, olives, coriander, scallions, and sesame seeds in a medium bowl. In a small bowl, whisk together lime juice, olive oil, soy sauce, and salt. Pour over rice mixture and toss. Serve at room temperature.

Makes 4 to 5 servings.

Cousin Ernie's
Country Fried Chicken

¼ cup (60 g) salt, preferably kosher
2 tablespoons freshly ground black pepper
4 tablespoons paprika
4 teaspoons garlic powder
1 teaspoon cayenne pepper
2 teaspoons ground ginger
2 to 3 pounds (1 to 1.5 kg) chicken, cut up
4 cups (920 g) plain yogurt
4 cups (540 g) all-purpose flour
corn oil

In a small bowl, combine salt, pepper, paprika, garlic powder, cayenne, and ginger. Using half of this mixture, rub spices all over chicken pieces, including under the skin. Put chicken pieces into a shallow container and cover with yogurt. Let sit at room temperature for ½ hour. Combine flour with remaining spice mixture. Heat 2 inches (5 cm) of corn oil in a large sauté pan over medium-low heat for about 10 minutes, or until it reaches 350°F (180°C). Remove chicken pieces from yogurt and coat in seasoned flour. Fry for about 20 minutes, or until crisp, brown, and cooked all the way through. Serve warm or at room temperature.

Makes 6 servings.

FRED: *Two other people wanted to buy this car.*
LUCY: *Where were they from . . . the Smithsonian Institute?*

Teensy and Weensy's Barbecued Ribs

5 pounds (2.25 kg) baby back ribs
1⅓ cups (320 ml) freshly squeezed orange juice
1⅓ cups (320 ml) rice wine vinegar
3 bay leaves
4 star anise
⅔ cup (160 g) hoisin sauce
½ cup (120 g) ketchup
3 tablespoons chopped garlic
2 teaspoons ground cumin
½ cup (20 g) chopped fresh coriander (cilantro)
4 scallions, including green part, chopped
2 tablespoons chopped fresh ginger
1 cup (240 g) drained crushed pineapple

Rinse ribs under cold water. Put into a large pot. Cover with cold water. Add ⅔ cup (160 ml) orange juice, ⅔ cup (160 ml) rice wine vinegar, bay leaves, and star anise. Bring to a boil, then continue to boil for 5 minutes. Meanwhile, combine hoisin sauce, ketchup, garlic, cumin, coriander, scallions, ginger, pineapple, and remaining orange juice and rice wine vinegar in a small bowl. Drain ribs and place in a shallow container. Pour barbecue sauce over ribs. Cover container with plastic wrap and let marinate at least 1 hour. Grill ribs over charcoal 15 to 20 minutes, turning frequently. Baste with barbecue sauce while grilling. Remove from grill, spoon remaining barbecue sauce over ribs, and serve immediately.

Makes 4 to 5 servings.

Tag-along Mertzes
Honey-Glazed Grilled Fruits

6 tablespoons unsalted butter, at room temperature
5 tablespoons honey
1/2 teaspoon black pepper
1/4 teaspoon ground nutmeg
1/4 teaspoon ground ginger
2 pounds (1 kg) assorted fruits such as pineapple,
papaya, cantaloupe, mango, pears, apricots, cherries,
nectarines, cut into 2-inch (5-cm) chunks
4 wooden skewers, soaked in water

*I*n a small bowl, combine butter, honey, pepper, nutmeg, and ginger with a wire whisk. Arrange fruit on the 4 skewers. Cook fruit kebabs on a grill for about 20 minutes, brushing with honey butter and turning frequently. Serve warm.

Makes 4 servings.

Visitor from Italy

Mario Gets a Little Taste of Cuba

LUCY: Yeah, what's the name of that new law, Ethel?

ETHEL: I don't know. You're the labor expert around here.

LUCY: It's called the, um, Taft-Hartley-Visitors-from-Italy-Who-Work-in-Pizzerias-Get-Every-Third-Day-Off Amendment.

MARIO: My goodness, America, she's a great country.

Mario's Cuban-Style Pizza

SWEET POTATO PIZZA CRUST
3½ cups (450 g) all-purpose flour
3 teaspoons baking powder
2 large eggs
½ cup (120 ml) olive oil
⅓ cup (80 ml) milk
¾ cup (230 g) cooked mashed sweet potato

PICADILLO TOPPING
¼ cup (60 ml) olive oil
1 yellow onion, diced
3 cloves garlic, finely minced
1¼ pounds (680 g) ground sirloin
2 cups (460 g) fresh chopped tomatoes or
drained and chopped canned tomatoes
½ teaspoon cayenne
1 teaspoon ground cumin
1 teaspoon salt
1 tablespoon Worcestershire sauce
½ teaspoon Tabasco sauce
½ cup (85 g) golden raisins
½ cup (75 g) pimento-stuffed olives

*P*reheat oven to 450°F (230°C) and place a baking sheet on the top rack. To make the crust, combine flour and baking powder in a large mixing bowl. Make a well in the center and add eggs, oil, and milk. Mix with a large spoon and then knead in the mashed potato. Knead for 10 minutes or pulse several minutes in a food processor until a smooth, elastic dough is formed. Roll out the dough on a lightly floured surface to ¼ inch (6 mm) thick. Cut out 3½-inch (9-cm) rounds with a cookie cutter or a glass or a sharp knife. To make topping, heat oil over medium-high heat and add onion and garlic. When translucent, add ground meat and cook until lightly browned, about 10 minutes. Lower heat and add tomatoes, cayenne, cumin, salt, Worcestershire, and Tabasco. Simmer 10 minutes and add raisins and olives and continue to simmer for several more minutes, until most of the liquid has evaporated. Remove baking sheet from oven and place rounds of dough on it. Generously spoon topping on each round. Bake for 10 minutes, until crust is lightly golden.

Makes about one dozen mini-pizzas.

Jalapeño Cheese Flan

½ recipe Sam Francesco Orange-Pepper Dough (p. 38)
3 eggs
1½ cups (360 ml) half-and-half
½ teaspoon salt
¼ teaspoon freshly ground black pepper
1 6-ounce (180-g) package jalapeño Monterey Jack cheese, grated or shredded
2 to 4 ounces (60 to 120 g) canned jalapeño peppers, chopped

Preheat oven to 350°F (180°C). On a floured surface, roll out dough to ¼ inch (6 mm) thick. Fit into a 9- or 10-inch (23- or 25-cm) tart pan with removable bottom or porcelain quiche dish. Place dish in freezer for at least ½ hour. Weight dough with aluminum foil filled with raw rice, beans, or pie weights. Bake for ½ hour. Remove foil and bake 5 minutes more, or until dough is lightly browned all the way through. Lower oven temperature to 325°F (165°C). Combine eggs, half-and-half, salt, and pepper with a wire whisk. Place shredded cheese evenly in tart shell along with chopped jalapeños (2 ounces of jalapeños make a spicy-hot flan; 4 ounces make it very spicy-hot). Pour egg mixture over until shell is filled. Place carefully in oven and bake 30 to 40 more minutes, or until custard is just set. Remove from oven and let cool. Cut into thin wedges and serve at room temperature.

Makes about 16 servings.

RICKY: *You and your bright ideas.*

LUCY: *What happened?*

RICKY: *Well, first of all, he thought that the nightclub was in a canal in Venice.*

LUCY: *What do you mean?*

RICKY: *He collected all the garbage and threw it out the window.*

LUCY: *Well, now that was an honest mistake.*

RICKY: *That's just the beginning. When I stopped singing Babalu, he stopped to applaud.*

LUCY: *Well, so what, I've seen busboys applaud before.*

RICKY: *While they're carrying a tray full of dishes?*

LUCY: *Well, he's not the first busboy that's ever dropped a tray full of dishes.*

RICKY: *Wait, wait, there's more.*

LUCY: *There's more?*

RICKY: *Yeah. As he bend over to clean the mess that he's made, the maitre d' was coming in with a cake for some newlyweds.*

LUCY: *Oh no!*

RICKY: *Yeah. He tripped over Mario, the whole thing went up in the air, and that bride and groom have the world's first upside-down wedding cake.*

Babalu Black Bean Dip

2 cups (540 g) cooked black beans
1 small onion
3 cloves garlic, peeled
1 cup (40 g) chopped fresh coriander (cilantro)
¼ cup (60 ml) olive oil
juice of 1 lime
1 tablespoon sherry wine vinegar
1 teaspoon ground cumin
½ teaspoon salt
½ teaspoon Worcestershire sauce
few drops Tabasco sauce

Combine beans, onion, garlic, and coriander in a food processor or blender and process until smooth. With motor running, add oil. Add remaining ingredients and process again until smooth. Serve with crackers, fresh vegetables, or plantain chips.

Makes about 3 cups (680 g).

Spicy Steamed Chicken Breasts

1¹/₂ ounces (45 g) meaty salt pork, chopped
2 medium cloves garlic, minced
1 medium onion (100 g), chopped
1 fresh chili pepper, seeded and chopped
1 whole boneless chicken breast (12 ounces/350 g), split
1 teaspoon ground cumin
¹/₂ teaspoon salt
¹/₄ teaspoon freshly ground black pepper
¹/₄ cup (60 ml) chicken broth or water

Heat a medium sauté pan over low heat. Add salt pork and sauté for 1 minute, then add garlic and onion and sauté for 4 to 5 minutes, stirring. Add chili pepper. Place chicken breast on top of onion mixture and sprinkle with cumin, salt, and pepper. Add broth or water to pan. Cook, covered, for 10 minutes. Remove contents of pan to a plate and let cool completely.

Makes 2 servings.

Mini-Cuban Sandwiches

4 ounces (120 g) chorizo sausages
1 small ripe avocado
juice of ½ lemon
2 tablespoons olive oil
½ teaspoon Tabasco sauce
salt and freshly ground black pepper
3 tablespoons mayonnaise
3 tablespoons chopped fresh coriander (cilantro)
½ chicken breast from
Spicy Steamed Chicken Breasts (p. 35)
1 loaf French or Italian bread
4 ounces (120 g) Swiss cheese, thinly sliced

Slice chorizo in half lengthwise, and then cook in a covered sauté pan with a little water. Let cool, then slice each half lengthwise into 3 long pieces. Meanwhile, peel and thinly slice avocado. Place slices on a plate and drizzle with lemon juice, 1 tablespoon of the olive oil, and the Tabasco sauce. Season with salt and pepper. Combine mayonnaise and coriander in a small bowl. Slice chicken breast into strips. Remove top and bottom crusts from the bread. Cut loaf into thirds crosswise, then slice each third in half lengthwise. Spread a little coriander mayonnaise on the inside of each piece of bread. Make a sandwich out of each third by layering chorizo, chicken strips, cheese, and avocado slices. Heat a large sauté pan over low heat. Add the remaining tablespoon of olive oil to the pan. Add the sandwiches and weight them down with a heavy pot lid or cast-iron weight, pressing them as much as possible. Sauté about 3 minutes on each side, or until well browned. Remove from pan and let cool 4 to 5 minutes. If serving as an hors d'oeuvre, cut each sandwich into 5 slices with a serrated knife.

Makes 15 hors d'oeuvres.

Martinelli's Hot and Spicy Stuffed Clams

2 dozen small cherrystone clams
1/3 cup (80 ml) beer or water
2 ounces (60 g) meaty salt pork, chopped
3 large cloves garlic, minced
1 cup (120 g) chopped onion
2 tablespoons capers, chopped
1/4 cup (30 g) bread crumbs
1 teaspoon Tabasco sauce
2 tablespoons olive oil
2 tablespoons clam liquid
1/4 cup (30 g) grated Parmesan cheese

Scrub clams, place in a large covered pot, and steam them in the beer or water until they open. Set aside to cool in their broth. Meanwhile, heat a sauté pan over low heat. Add salt pork and sauté until the fat is rendered and the bits of pork are crisp. Remove with a slotted spoon and reserve. Add garlic and onion to pan and sauté slowly for 5 minutes, or until golden. Remove from heat. Add capers, bread crumbs, Tabasco sauce, olive oil, and 2 tablespoons of the clam broth. Combine well. Remove the clams from their shells and chop them very coarsely. Add these to the bread crumb mixture along with the bits of crispy salt pork. (Remove any excess fat from the bits first.) Stuff the clam shells, mounding each shell with the mixture and pressing to compact it. Place the clams on a baking sheet or broiler pan. Preheat broiler. Sprinkle stuffed clams with Parmesan cheese and broil for 1 minute, or until cheese is bubbly. Serve immediately.

Makes about 1 dozen stuffed clams.

Sam Francesco
Orange-Pepper Dough

12 tablespoons (180 g) cold unsalted butter plus
12 tablespoons (180 g) lard
(or use all cold unsalted butter)
4 cups (480 g) all-purpose flour
1½ teaspoons salt
1½ teaspoons freshly ground black pepper
grated zest of 2 oranges (about 2 teaspoons)
½ cup (120 ml) freshly squeezed orange juice
2 eggs

*D*ice butter and lard if using. Sift flour, salt, and pepper onto work surface. Cut butter into flour with fingertips or a pastry cutter until mixture resembles coarse salt. Whisk together rind, orange juice, and egg in a small bowl. Add egg mixture to flour mixture and combine until a dough is formed. Wrap dough in plastic and chill before using.

Makes about 18 3½-inch (9-cm) rounds.

DOMINIC: *They tell me Mario is staying here.*
RICKY: *Well, Mario was here but he's on his way to California.*
DOMINIC: *California?*
LUCY: *Yes, he found out that his brother Dominic moved to San Francisco.*
DOMINIC: *Mamma mia, but I'm his brother Dominic.*
LUCY & RICKY: *You. You are?*
DOMINIC: *I don't move to San Francisco, I just go stay with my sick friend Sam Francesco.*

Dominic's Chicken and Rice Empanadas

½ chicken breast from
Spicy Steamed Chicken Breasts (p. 35)
½ cup (100 g) cooked rice
½ cup (75 g) chopped pimento-stuffed green olives
½ teaspoon ground cumin
½ teaspoon Tabasco sauce
1 teaspoon lime juice
1 recipe Sam Francesco Orange-Pepper Dough (p. 38)
egg wash (1 egg mixed with 1 tablespoon milk)

*P*reheat oven to 350°F (180°C). Chop chicken breast with some of the onions from steaming and place in a small bowl. Add rice, olives, cumin, Tabasco, and lime juice. Combine well. Roll dough out to ⅛ inch (3 mm) thick. Cut out 3½-inch (9-cm) rounds of dough with a round cookie cutter or a glass. Put a heaping tablespoon of filling onto each round of dough. Brush the edge of the dough with egg wash and then fold the dough over to make a half moon shape. Press to seal edges and then use the tines of a fork to seal and decorate edge. Place the empanadas on a baking sheet lined with parchment or wax paper and bake for 15 to 20 minutes, or until they are a light golden brown. Serve warm or at room temperature.

Makes about 18 empanadas.

Lucy Does a TV Commercial

Cocktails at the Tropicana

LUCY: Hello, friends, I'm your Vitameatavegamin girl. Are you tired, run down, listless? Do you poop out at parties? Are you unpopular? The answer to all your problems is in this little bottle.

ROSS: Now you pick up the bottle.

LUCY: Oh.

ROSS: Little higher. That's right.

LUCY: The answer to all your problems is in this little bottle. Vitameatavegamin. Vitameatavegamin contains vitamins, meat, vegetables, and minerals. Yes, with Vitameatavegamin you can spoon your way to health. All you do is take a tablespoonful after every meal.

ROSS: Now you take some.

LUCY: Oh. It's so tasty, too. It's just like candy.

ROSS: No, no, no, no. You're supposed to like the stuff. Smile, be happy. Now try it again.

Vitameatavegamin

1 small peeled cucumber (8 ounces/230 g),
coarsely chopped
1 red bell pepper (6 ounces/180 g)
1 cup (240 ml) tomato juice
3 drops Tabasco sauce
4 drops Worcestershire sauce
1 teaspoon prepared horseradish
2 teaspoons Rose's lime juice
¾ cup (180 ml) vodka

Hold pepper over a medium-high flame to blacken skin, then peel under running water. In a food processor, combine cucumber and red pepper by pulsing until a purée is obtained. Mix purée with remaining ingredients. Pour into a tall chilled glass filled with ice.

Makes 4 drinks.

A good deal of time and effort was expended by stage manager Herb Browar to find just the right liquid concoction to fill the Vitameatavegamin bottles. It had to ooze out of the bottle, not flow freely, plus it had to taste good to Lucy. After trying and dismissing a half-dozen products, including honey, Browar stopped off at a health food store and found the perfect liquid: apple pectin.
(From Bart Andrews, The "I Love Lucy" Book, Doubleday, 1985.)

ROSS: This stuff any good?
JOE: Well, it ought to be. It's got everything in it. Meat, vegetables, minerals, alcohol 23%. Alcohol 23%!

Mambo Martini

2 cups (500 ml) vodka
1¼ cups (290 g) peeled sliced pineapple
1 jalapeño pepper, seeded and sliced
¼ cup (60 ml) pineapple juice

*I*n a pitcher or other glass container, combine vodka, pineapple slices, and jalapeño. Cover and let set 24 to 48 hours. Add pineapple juice and ice cubes. Stir vigorously and then strain into 4 chilled martini glasses.

Makes 4 drinks.

Crazy Cuban Coconut Coffee

1½ cups (150 g) unsweetened coconut (see note below)
1½ cups (360 ml) milk
¾ cup (60 g) espresso beans
shot of rum (optional)

Preheat oven to 400°F (200°C). Spread coconut on baking sheet and bake until it has turned dark brown, 12 to 15 minutes. It should be stirred a few times during baking to prevent burning edges. Meanwhile, heat milk in a small saucepan. Add half of the toasted coconut to milk. Remove from heat and allow to steep. In a coffee grinder, grind remaining coconut with espresso beans. Prepare coffee using 2 tablespoons of the coconut-coffee grinds per cup of coffee. Strain coconut milk, then reheat gently. Serve coffee with warm coconut milk and a shot of rum, if desired.

Note: Unsweetened desiccated coconut can be purchased at natural foods stores.

Makes 4 drinks.

Havana Banana

3 ounces (80 ml) dark rum
2 ounces (60 ml) chocolate liqueur, such as Godiva
1 ounce (30 ml) crème de banane
1 ounce (30 ml) milk
cinnamon (optional)

Fill a large glass with ice. Add all the ingredients and shake until well blended. Strain into a chilled cocktail glass. Sprinkle with cinnamon if desired.

Makes 1 drink.

Frozen Guava Daiquiri

2¼ cups (550 ml) guava nectar
½ cup (120 ml) white rum
¼ cup (60 ml) Rose's lime juice
1 tablespoon confectioners' (icing) or
superfine (caster) sugar
fresh lime slices for garnish

Freeze 1¾ cups (420 ml) guava nectar in an ice cube tray. In a blender, combine guava ice cubes, remaining guava nectar, rum, lime juice, and sugar. Process until homogeneous. Pour into chilled martini or margarita glasses and garnish with fresh lime slices.

Makes 4 drinks.

Rum-ba Royale

1 medium papaya (about 12 ounces/350 g),
peeled, seeded, and chopped
1 cup (240 ml) papaya nectar
1 bottle (750 ml) champagne
dark rum
strawberry slices for garnish

*P*urée papaya with papaya nectar in a blender. For each drink, pour 3 ounces (80 ml) champagne into a chilled champagne glass. Add 2 ounces (60 ml) puréed papaya. Top with a splash of rum. Garnish with a sliced strawberry.

Makes 8 drinks.

LUCY: *Do you pop out at parties? Are you unpoopular? Well, are you?*

Flaming Redhead

2 ounces (60 ml) gin
1 ounce (30 ml) freshly squeezed orange juice
1 ounce (30 ml) cranberry juice
1 tablespoon Grand Marnier
club soda
grenadine
fresh orange slice

*I*n a tall glass filled with ice, pour gin, orange juice, cranberry juice, and Grand Marnier. Add a splash of club soda. Drizzle grenadine on top. Stir. Garnish with an orange slice.

Makes 1 drink.

LUCY: *Vitameatavegamin contains vitamins, meat, megatables, and vinerals.*

Tropicana Teaser

3¼ cups (780 ml) peach nectar
¾ cup (180 ml) dark rum
½ cup (120 ml) peach schnapps
2 fresh peaches, peeled, pitted, and sliced
¼ cup (60 ml) heavy cream

*F*reeze 1¾ cups (420 ml) peach nectar in an ice cube tray. In a blender, combine peach ice cubes, remaining peach nectar, rum, peach schnapps, and 1 fresh peach. Process until ice is crushed. Add heavy cream and continue to blend until the mixture is creamy and homogeneous. Pour into chilled white wine glasses or champagne flutes and garnish with fresh peach slices.

Makes 4 to 5 drinks.

Mango Colada

1 tablespoon cream of coconut
1 tablespoon lime juice
¾ cup (180 g) crushed ice
¼ cup (60 ml) puréed mango
1 ounce (30 ml) light rum

*P*lace all ingredients in a blender and blend until a smooth consistency is reached.

Makes 1 drink.

Job Switching

Sweets from the Chocolate Factory

RICKY: Hey listen, by the way, what do you know about rice?

FRED: Well, I had it thrown at me on one of the darkest days of my life.

RICKY: I mean how much do you think we should use for four people?

FRED: Well, I don't know. People like that stuff.

RICKY: Well, how does one pound per person sound?

FRED: That sounds about right.

For "Job Switching" Amanda Milligan, a candy dipper at See's Candy factory, was hired for the chocolate dipping sequence. Jess Oppenheimer recalls her first encounter with Lucy, who asked her if she liked the show. "What show," the woman answered. Lucy replied, "'I Love Lucy.'" The dipper asked, "When is it on?" and Lucy answered, "Monday night." "Oh," said the woman, "I watch wrestling that night." (From Bart Andrews, The "I Love Lucy" Book, Doubleday, 1985.)

Kramer's Kandy Krispies

8 ounces (230 g) bittersweet, semisweet, or milk chocolate, melted
2 tablespoons toasted coconut
½ cup (85 g) chopped golden raisins
1 cup (25 g) crispy rice cereal
1 cup (45 g) chopped marshmallows

Combine all ingredients in a small bowl. Fill a self-sealing freezer bag with mixture. Snip off a corner of the freezer bag. Squeeze out logs of the mixture, ¾ inch (2 cm) wide by 3½ inches (9 cm) long, onto a baking sheet lined with parchment or wax paper. Chill in refrigerator or freezer until chocolate is firm.

Makes 2 dozen candies.

SUPERVISOR: *Ricardo, I'm going to put you to work chocolate dipping. You say you've had experience?*
LUCY: *Oh, yes ma'am, yes ma'am. I'm a dipper from way back.*
SUPERVISOR: *Yes?*
LUCY: *They used to call me the big dipper.*
SUPERVISOR: *There's no room in this plant for levity, however weak.*

Honey Dipped Pecan Truffles

FILLING

½ cup (120 ml) heavy cream
2 tablespoons (30 g) unsalted butter
½ cup (150 g) honey
8 ounces (230 g) bittersweet chocolate, finely chopped

COATING

1 cup (120 g) chopped pecans
¼ cup (75 g) honey
12 ounces (350 g) bittersweet chocolate, finely chopped

To make filling, in a small saucepan, combine cream, butter, and honey. Bring to a boil slowly, then remove mixture from heat and immediately add chocolate. Stir slowly with a wire whisk until chocolate is melted and mixture is homogeneous. Transfer to a bowl and let mixture cool at room temperature 1 hour. Drop mixture by well rounded tablespoons onto a baking sheet lined with parchment or wax paper. Chill until firm. Remove tray from refrigerator and quickly roll each spoonful of chocolate filling into a ball about ½ inch (13 mm) in diameter. (It's helpful to coat hands lightly with cocoa powder every so often). Return pan to refrigerator. To make coating, preheat oven to 400°F (200°C). Spread pecans on a baking sheet and drizzle with honey. Bake for 15 minutes, or until pecans are toasted and honey is bubbling. Let cool, then chop mixture finely. Put into a round container such as a cake pan. Melt remaining chocolate by putting it into a small, clean, dry bowl. Put bowl over a small saucepan of gently simmering water (make sure bowl fits snugly over saucepan). Stir chocolate slowly until it melts, then remove bowl from saucepan. Remove tray of chocolate balls from refrigerator. Using 2 forks, dip each chocolate ball into the melted chocolate. Scrape bottom of forks along edge of bowl to remove excess chocolate. Then place ball into pan of chopped nuts. Swirl container of nuts in a circular motion to coat truffle completely. Remove each truffle to a clean tray after it is coated.

Makes about 75 truffles.

LUCY: *I write a check to the beauty parlor every month.*
RICKY: *Yes, I know that, but they don't always have a little note in the back like this one. "Dear teller, be a lamb and don't put this through till next month." Now what do you got to say for yourself?*
LUCY: *That's why they call 'em tellers, they go around blabbing everything they know.*

Raspberry Chocolate Lace Cookies

½ cup (120 g) unsalted butter
¾ cup (120 g) brown sugar
½ cup (180 g) dark corn syrup
½ cup (60 g) all-purpose flour
1 cup (90 g) rolled oats
2 ounces (60 g) bittersweet chocolate, melted

FILLING
4 ounces (120 g) chocolate, melted
¾ cup (180 g) raspberry preserves

*P*reheat oven to 350°F (180°C). In a small saucepan, melt butter over medium heat. Whisk in brown sugar and corn syrup. Bring to a boil, whisking frequently. Turn heat to low and whisk in flour. Bring to a boil again, whisking constantly. Remove from heat and stir in oats and the melted chocolate. Let mixture cool to room temperature. Meanwhile, butter a baking sheet and sprinkle lightly with flour. Roll batter into ½-inch (13-mm) or olive-sized balls. Place balls 3 inches (7.5 cm) apart on baking sheet. Bake for 4 to 5 minutes. Cookies will spread out and form flat, lacy discs. Let cookies cool slightly on sheet, then carefully remove from sheet with a spatula. Spread 1 cookie with a small amount of melted chocolate, then spread another with a small amount of jam. Put the 2 cookies together to make a sandwich.

Makes about 40 to 45 cookies.

Chocolate Peanut Butter Wrap

8 ounces (230 g) bittersweet or semisweet chocolate
1/2 cup (120 ml) heavy cream
10 sheets phyllo dough
1 1/2 cups (360 g) unsalted butter, melted
1/4 cup (45 g) confectioners' sugar
1/4 cup (60 g) peanut butter
1/4 cup (60 g) chopped peanuts, lightly toasted

*P*reheat oven to 350°F (180°C). Chop chocolate finely and place in a small bowl. Bring heavy cream slowly to a boil. When cream boils, pour over chocolate. Stir with a wire whisk until smooth. Set aside. Lay sheets of phyllo flat and keep them covered with a damp cloth while working. Lay 1 sheet of phyllo on a work surface. Brush with melted butter and sprinkle with confectioners' sugar. Lay a second sheet of phyllo on top of the first sheet. Repeat with butter and confectioners' sugar. With a sharp knife, cut phyllo into 5 strips, each 3 inches (7.5 cm) wide by 12 inches (30.5 cm) long. At the top of each strip, place a rounded teaspoonful of chocolate filling plus 1/4 teaspoon of peanut butter and 1/4 teaspoon of chopped peanuts. Fold one corner over filling to make a triangle shape. Then fold up the strip like a flag. Brush the finished triangles with melted butter and sprinkle with confectioners' sugar. Repeat until all of the filling is used. Place triangles on a baking sheet lined with parchment or wax paper. Bake for 13 to 15 minutes, or until light golden brown.

Makes about 25 triangles.

FRED: *I brought my cake, seven layers of luscious devil's food. Wait till you see it.*

RICKY: *What happened to the other six layers?*

FRED: *They're all in there. Some of 'em just didn't rise very much.*

RICKY: *Well, you can put on a lot of frosting.*

FRED: *What do you mean put on? The frosting's all ready in it.*

RICKY: *In it?*

FRED: *Yeah, I mixed it all up together before I baked the cake.*

RICKY: *Well, maybe you better wait until breakfast and serve it as a pancake.*

LUCY: *What are you doing up here? I thought you were downstairs boxing chocolates.*

ETHEL: *Oh, they kicked me out of there fast.*

LUCY: *Why?*

ETHEL: *I kept pinching 'em to see what kind they were.*

Conveyor Belt Cranberry Brownies

¾ cup (90 g) dried cranberries
½ cup (120 ml) freshly squeezed orange juice
12 ounces (345 g) bittersweet chocolate
1 cup (240 g) unsalted butter
6 eggs
¾ teaspoon salt
2 cups (480 g) sugar
1¼ cups (150 g) flour
¼ cup (30 g) cocoa powder
1 cup (90 g) walnuts

Preheat oven to 350°F (180°C). In a small nonaluminum sauce-pan, combine dried cranberries and orange juice. Heat until juice begins to boil. Remove from heat and set aside. Butter a 9- or 10-inch (23- or 25-cm) square baking dish or pan. Chop all of the chocolate in chunks about ½ inch (13 mm) square. Reserve ¼ of the chopped chocolate to add to batter later. Melt the remaining 8 ounces (230 g) of chocolate along with the butter in a small bowl set over a pot of gently simmering water. (Water should not touch bottom of bowl.) Stir with a wire whisk until homogeneous and then set aside. In a large bowl, beat eggs with salt and sugar until mixture is pale yellow. Add chocolate mixture and combine well. Stir in flour and cocoa. Then add choco-late chunks, walnuts, and cranberry–orange juice mixture. Pour batter into prepared pan. Bake for about 35 to 40 minutes, or until toothpick inserted in center comes out coated with moist crumbs. Cool completely. Cut into squares.

Makes about 24 brownies.

L.A.
at Last

Desserts at the Brown Derby

LUCY: Well, I spose we could just drive up and down the streets and hunt movie stars.

FRED: Why not!

LUCY: Although tracking 'em down one by one takes so much time. I wonder if there's any place they get together in a big herd.

FRED: Well, maybe at sundown they all gather at the same watering hole.

LUCY: That's it! That's where we'll go.

ETHEL: Where?

LUCY: The watering hole. Fellow hunters, we're going to the Brown Derby.

Richard Widmark's Orange and Grapefruit Granita

1½ cups (360 g) sugar
1½ cups (360 ml) water
2 cups (500 ml) freshly squeezed orange juice
2 cups (500 ml) freshly squeezed grapefruit juice
1⅓ cups (320 ml) champagne or sparkling wine
1 pint (12 ounces/350 g) fresh strawberries
½ cup (120 ml) Grand Marnier

Combine sugar and water in a small saucepan. Bring to a boil and then remove from heat. Let cool completely. Combine orange juice, grapefruit juice, and champagne. Add sugar syrup and strain into a wide, shallow container. Place container in freezer and allow to freeze completely. At least 10 minutes before serving, slice strawberries and toss with 2 tablespoons Grand Marnier in a small bowl. Cover bowl with plastic wrap and let marinate for 10 minutes or more. To serve, remove granita from freezer and scrape shavings from it with a large metal spoon. Place sliced strawberries in the bottoms of each of 6 chilled red wine glasses or goblets. Add shavings of granita and drizzle remaining Grand Marnier over shavings.

Note: The granita should be made a day or at least 8 hours in advance to allow enough time to freeze completely.

Makes 6 servings.

WAITER: *All right now, have you decided what you're going to have?*
LUCY: *It's so hard to decide. Everything is so tempting. What is this derby tossed salad?*
FRED: *Anybody knows that, Lucy. You just take some salad and toss it in a derby.*

Dore Schary's
Mixed Berry Shortcakes

1½ cups (180 g) plus 1 tablespoon (250 g) all-purpose flour
3½ tablespoons sugar
2¼ teaspoons baking powder
¼ teaspoon baking soda
¼ teaspoon salt
½ cup (120 g) cold unsalted butter,
cut into ½-inch (13-mm) pieces
1 cup (240 g) plain yogurt
1 teaspoon grated orange zest
3 tablespoons fresh orange juice
1½ cups (360 ml) plus 1 tablespoon heavy cream
½ pint (6 ounces/180 g) fresh strawberries, sliced
½ pint (5 ounces/150 g) fresh raspberries
½ pint (5 ounces/150 g) fresh blackberries

Preheat oven to 375°F (190°C). Sift flour, 1½ tablespoons sugar, baking powder, baking soda, and salt onto work surface. Cut in butter until mixture resembles coarse meal. Make a well in mixture and add ½ cup (120 g) yogurt, orange zest, and 1 tablespoon orange juice. Mix with hands until a soft dough is formed. Roll out dough to ½ inch (13 mm) thick. Cut out 3-inch (7.5-cm) rounds with a cookie cutter or the top of a glass. Place rounds on a baking sheet lined with parchment or wax paper. Brush shortcakes with 1 tablespoon heavy cream and sprinkle with 1 tablespoon sugar. Bake for 12 to 14 minutes, or until lightly browned. Meanwhile, in a small bowl, combine all berries with remaining tablespoon of sugar and remaining 2 tablespoons of orange juice. Cover bowl with plastic wrap and set aside. In a large chilled bowl, beat 1½ cups heavy cream with remaining ½ cup of yogurt until soft peaks have formed. Keep mixture chilled until ready to use. To serve, cut warm shortcakes in half. Place bottom half on plate, spoon some of the berry mixture over, then place a mound of yogurt–whipped cream over berries. Place remaining half of shortcake on top.

Makes 6 servings.

The Duke's Rice and Apricot Dream

1 cup (150 g) dark brown sugar
⅓ cup (60 g) rice
4 cups (1 liter) half-and-half
1 tablespoon sugar
½ vanilla bean
pinch of nutmeg
2 egg yolks
¾ cup (170 g) Preserved Apricots (see following recipe)

Spread out brown sugar on a baking sheet. Let dry out at least 2 hours, then press with fingers through a sieve. Set aside. Blanch rice in boiling water for 1 minute. Rinse under cold water. Combine rice, 3 cups (750 ml) of the half-and-half, sugar, seeds from vanilla bean, and nutmeg in a medium saucepan. Bring to a boil, then cook over low heat until rice is very soft, about 50 minutes to 1 hour. Stir rice frequently during this period. Remove pot from heat. Preheat oven to 325°F (165°C). Let rice cool slightly, then stir in the remaining half-and-half and the egg yolks. Spoon a small amount of preserved apricots into the bottom of 6 4-ounce (120-ml) ramekins. Fill ramekins ½ to ¾ full with rice mixture. Put ramekins into an ovenproof container such as a roasting pan. Fill roasting pan with warm water until the water comes halfway up the side of the ramekins. Bake 35 to 40 minutes, or until custard is just set. Remove from oven and chill. When custard is firm, remove from refrigerator and sprinkle top evenly with brown sugar. Place under broiler and broil until sugar is bubbly, 1 to 2 minutes. Serve immediately.

Makes 6 servings.

Preserved Apricots

**12 fresh apricots (600 g), pitted and halved
1¼ cups (300 g) sugar
juice of 1 lemon**

 C ombine apricots, sugar, and lemon juice in a small bowl.
Cover with plastic wrap and let marinate 2 hours at room temperature. Transfer apricots to a small nonaluminum saucepan
and cook over low heat for 1 to 1½ hours. Remove preserves to a
clean container and chill.

Makes about 4 cups (900 g).

LUCY: *Look at the salads!*
ETHEL: *Look at the pastries!*
FRED: *Look at the prices!*

Hedda Hopper's
Chocolate Coconut Chapeau

1 loaf (170 g) day-old Italian or French bread,
sliced in half lengthwise
6 tablespoons (90 g) unsalted butter, melted
3 cups (750 ml) half-and-half
4 egg yolks
½ cup (120 g) sugar
1 teaspoon vanilla extract
1 cup (100 g) shredded sweetened coconut
1 cup (240 ml) milk
1 cup (170 g) chocolate chips
or chopped bittersweet chocolate

CHOCOLATE SAUCE
1 cup (240 ml) milk
4 ounces (120 g) bittersweet chocolate, chopped
1 tablespoon unsalted butter
1 tablespoon rum

*P*reheat oven to 400°F (200°C). Place bread in oven for 5 minutes, or until it just starts to color. Remove from oven, let cool slightly, and then crumble it into a large bowl. Add melted butter and toss well. Lower oven temperature to 325°F (165°C). Add half-and-half to bread and let sit 5 to 10 minutes. In a small bowl, whisk together egg yolks, sugar, and vanilla. Add egg mixture to the soaked bread, then add coconut, milk, and chocolate. Spoon mixture into 8 buttered 4-ounce (120-ml) ramekins. Place ramekins in a shallow ovenproof container such as a roasting pan, then fill pan with enough hot water to come halfway up the sides of the ramekins. Bake for 25 to 30 minutes, or until mixture is set. Remove ramekins from roasting pan and let cool to room temperature. To make chocolate sauce, bring milk to a boil and then stir in chocolate, butter, and rum. Remove from heat and stir until homogenous. Keep warm until ready to serve. When ready to serve "chapeaus," run a knife around inside of each ramekin and unmold onto a pool of chocolate sauce.

Makes 8 chapeaus.

Cornel Wilde's Cabernet Sabayon

⅓ cup (90 g) sugar
⅔ cup (160 ml) cabernet sauvignon
1 cinnamon stick, split in half lengthwise
6 egg yolks
½ cup (120 ml) heavy cream, whipped
6 to 8 fresh figs, sliced
4 plums, sliced
4 nectarines, sliced

Combine sugar, wine, and cinnamon stick in a small saucepan. Meanwhile put egg yolks into a medium bowl. When wine mixture comes to a boil, start beating egg yolks with an electric mixer. After wine mixture has boiled for 3 minutes, pour in a thin stream into egg yolks, continuously beating. Beat until mixture triples in volume and is cool. Fold whipped cream into sabayon. Chill at least 10 minutes. Meanwhile, divide fruit slices among 6 to 8 large wine glasses. Before serving, spoon sabayon over fruit. Alternately, a gratin can be made by arranging fruit on individual ovenproof plates or crème brûlée dishes. Spoon sabayon over fruit and put under broiler for 30 seconds, or until sabayon browns. Serve immediately.

Makes 6 to 8 servings.

Harpo Marx's Rum-Soaked Macadamia Pound Cake

$^1/_2$ cup (120 g) unsalted butter, at room temperature
$^3/_4$ cup (180 g) sugar
2 eggs
$^1/_2$ cup (120 g) sour cream
1 teaspoon vanilla extract
$^1/_2$ teaspoon almond extract
$1^1/_2$ cups (180 g) all-purpose flour
$^3/_4$ teaspoon baking powder
$^1/_4$ teaspoon salt
$^3/_4$ cup (120 g) coarsely chopped fresh pineapple
or fresh cherries
$^3/_4$ cup (120 g) coarsely chopped macadamia nuts

SYRUP
$^1/_2$ cup (120 ml) dark rum
$^1/_2$ cup (120 g) sugar
$^1/_4$ cup (60 ml) water

*P*reheat oven to 325°F (165°C). In a large bowl, cream butter
and sugar with an electric mixer until extremely light and fluffy.
Add eggs one at a time. Then add sour cream. Scrape down sides
of bowl with a plastic spatula. Add extracts. Combine well. Stir in
flour, baking powder, baking soda, and salt until homogeneous.
Stir in pineapple or cherries and nuts. Turn batter into a buttered
and floured 5-cup (1.2-liter) loaf pan. Bake for about 1 hour, or until toothpick inserted in center of cake comes out clean. When cake
is almost done, combine ingredients for syrup in a small saucepan
and bring to a boil. Remove from heat. When cake comes out of
the oven, poke holes in the top of it with a wooden skewer or toothpick. Brush on the warm syrup and let it soak through the cake.
Invert cake onto a rack and repeat process on the bottom and sides
of the cake, until syrup is used up. Serve at room temperature.

Makes 1 loaf cake.